SEROTONIN NATURALLY

5-HTP is a little-known, but well-tested, dietary supplement that offers many people more benefits and less risks than most conventional therapies for depression, sleep disorders including insomnia, obesity, anxiety disorders including panic attacks, PMS, eating disorders including bulimia, obsessive-compulsive disorders, alcholism, and uncontrollable violent impulses. We will explain how 5-HTP works and how to use it correctly as a dietary supplement. Hopefully it will help make your life, and the lives of those you love, more pleasant.

Richard A. Passwater, Ph.D. is one of the most called-upon authorities in preventive health care. A noted biochemist, he is credited with popularizing the term "supernutrition" in such books as *Supernutrition: Megavitamin Revolution* and *The New Supernutrition*. His many other works include *Cancer Prevention and Nutritional Therapies* and *Pycnogenol*. Dr. Passwater lives in Berlin, Maryland, where he is the director of a research laboratory.

James South, M.A. has been a nutrition consultant, writer, lecturer and teacher for 25 years. He was director of research and product formulator for one of America's major vitamin companies from 1987 to 1995. His master's degree is in the philosophy of biology, psychology and medicine. He is currently serving as director of research for an international antiaging clinic opening in Europe in 1998.

5-HTP: The Natural Serotonin Solution

Gain all the health benefits your brain needs with a natural serotonin booster

Richard A. Passwater, Ph.D.
and James South, M.A.

KEATS PUBLISHING

LOS ANGELES

NTC/Contemporary Publishing Group

5-HTP

Copyright © 1998 by Richard A. Passwater and James South

ISBN: 0-87983-939-2

Printed in the United States of America

06 07 08 09 RCP 9 8 7 6

CONTENTS

INTRODUCTION

A large body of evidence derived from human clinical trials and animal experiments conducted over the past 35 years indicates that 5-HTP (5-hydroxytryptophan) may be useful for a broad range of health problems. Depression, anxiety disorders, panic attacks, alcoholism, PMS, obesity, eating disorders such as bulimia, obsessive-compulsive disorders, insomnia and uncontrollable violent impulses have all been treated with, or show evidence of underlying brain dysfunction which might be improved by, 5-HTP. Ironically, however, 5-HTP itself does not directly perform any specific function in the body. 5-HTP's only known role is to serve as the precursor, or raw material, which some cells use to create the neurotransmitter serotonin. So in a very real sense, that story of 5-HTP is really the "serotonin story."

Serotonin is one of a dozen or so major brain neurotransmitters. Serotinin is also used by some cells outside the brain. Ninety percent of the body's serotonin-using neurons are found in the intestinal tract, where serotonin helps regulate peristalsis and digestion. Only about 1 percent of serotonin nerve cells are found in the brain, where they make up about 0.01 percent of the brain's 10–100 billion neurons. The brain serotonin nerve cells are mostly found in a group called "the raphe nuclei." This cluster of neurons is situated in the pons and brainstem, structures that have been referred to as part of the "deep basement of the brain." The serotonin neurons send out wirelike projections to virtually every other area of the brain—the cortex, limbic system, hypothalamus and thalamus, as well as the spinal cord. Each neuron may connect to as many as 10,000 other nerve cells. Yet these interconnecting neurons do not quite touch each other—there is a microscopic gap between them called the "synaptic gap." As a burst of electric current travels down the length of a neuron, it releases a packet of neurotransmitter molecules stored at the edge of the neuron.

These neurotransmitters then diffuse across the synaptic gap and "plug in" to the receptor sites of the next neuron, like keys fitting into locks. When a sufficient number of molecules have "plugged in" to the receptors of the next neuron, this neuron then discharges a burst of electricity down its cell-membrane surface, repeating the process with neurons to which it connects. Thus neurons use electricity to transmit information down the length of their own cell structure, but use chemical neurotransmitter molecules to signal other neurons. Neurotransmitters are thus the means whereby nerve cells "talk" to each other. When there are inadequate numbers of neurotransmitters to activate other neurons, various brain circuits may become under- or overactive due to lack of communication between nerve cells.

Studies with humans and animals have shown that serotonin nerve circuits promote feelings of well-being, calmness, personal security, relaxation and confidence. Serotonin neural circuits also help counterbalance the tendency of dopamine and noradrenalin (another neurotransmitter and a hormone) neural circuits to encourage overarousal, fear, anger, tension, aggression, violence, overeating, anxiety and insomnia when they become overactivated, perhaps due to stress, danger or overstimulation.[1]

Serontonin, dopamine and noradrenalin (also called norepinephrine) are the three main "monoamine" neurotransmitters ("monamine" refers to the chemical structure of the molecules). They are each made from one specific amino acid. Amino acids are the building blocks of protein molecules such as neurotransmitters and enzymes. Serotonin is made from tryptophan, while dopamine and noradrenalin are made from tyrosine. While some blood components such as blood platelets and cells outside the brain such as intestinal neurons make and/or use serotonin, all serotonin used by brain cells must be made within the neurons that use serotonin. Due to the "blood-brain barrier," no serontonin can be "imported" from outside the brain. The blood-brain barrier serves as a two-stage protective device to prevent toxins from entering the brain. It also protects brain function from being disturbed by temporary surges of nutrients in the blood following meals. Even molecules needed by the brain, such as amino acids, are limited in their access to the brain. Nutrients are ferried through the blood-brain barrier by special transport molecules, like passengers on a bus.

Until the late 1960s, neuroscientists assumed that the brain's supply of its neurotransmitters was controlled directly by the brain, independently of dietary or blood levels of the precursor nutrients needed to make neurotransmitters. The pioneering work of Massachusetts Institute of Technology (MIT) scientists John Fernstrom and Richard Wurtman throughout the 1970s dispelled this long-held "neuro-myth." Working initially with rats, Fernstrom and Wurtman discovered that the level of neurotransmitter precursor nutrients contained in a meal could directly affect the synthesis of neurotransmitters in the brain. Four neurotransmitters—serotonin, dopamine, noradrenalin and acetylcholine—were found to be under "precursor control." This meant that dietary consumption patterns could strongly affect the level of production of neurotransmitters in the brain. Dopamine, noradrenalin and acetylcholine were found to be under "weak precursor control". Although dietary levels of their precursor nutrients could affect brain synthesis of these neurotransmitters, the effect only became pronounced when the nerves using them were firing rapidly, as under great stress, exertion, or danger. Serotonin, however, was found to be under strong precursor control—the synthesis level of serotonin was directly tied to the availability of tryptophan in brain cells, independently of whether the serotonin nerves were quiescent or furiously active. This provided the first evidence that serotonin-activated neural circuits might be the brain's Achilles' heel—a potential weak spot in optimal brain function.

Throughout the 1970s scientists discovered a number of factors that confirmed serotinin production to be a major potential weak link in brain biochemistry. Serotonin's precursor, tryptophan, is one of 20 amino acids provided in food. It is one of the eight "essential amino acids." Unlike "nonessential" amino acids which can be made in the body as needed, the essential amino acids must be taken in preformed from the diet—the body cannot make them. In any normal diet—animal-protein based or vegetarian—tryptophan is the least plentiful of all 20 food amino acids. The typical daily diet provides only about 750–1,500 mg (milligrams) of tryptophan. Besides serotonin manufacture, tryptophan has many possible metabolic fates. Some of it is used to make protein. Some is used by the liver to make the active form of the B vitamin, niacin (vitamin B3). The active form is called nicotine adenine dinucleotide (NAD), and 60 mg of tryptophan is used up for each 1–2 mg of NAD that is made. A liver enzyme called "tryptophan pyrrolase" breaks down some tryptophan into waste metabolities (by-products) such as kynurenine and xanthurenic acid as soon as tryptophan enters the liver from the digestive tract. It is generally estimated that less than 1 percent of ingested tryptophan ever makes it to the brain for serotonin production. And to make matters worse, tryptophan must share the transport molecule used to get through the blood-brain barrier with five other competing large neutral amino acids (LNAA). The competing LNAAs are phenylalanine, tyrosine, valine, leucine and isoleucine.

The determining factor in how much tryptophan gets into the brain is not the absolute level of tryptophan in the blood—it is rather the ratio of tryptophan to the sum total of the other competing LNAAs in the blood. Under normal conditions, this ratio ranges from 0.065 to 0.16, meaning that there will only be one fifteenth to one sixth as much tryptophan as its competitors. Ironically, the tryptophan ratio will tend to be highest after a high carbohydrate/low protein meal, and lowest after a high protein meal. Even though a high protein meal will provide more tryptophan than a low protein meal, it will provide proportionately even more of the competing LNAAs—so the tryptophan ratio drops after a high protein meal. This means that the best way to absorb tryptophan without competition from LNAAs is to ingest it without other proteins and with carbohydrates.

When a high carbohydrate meal is eaten, this will normally lead to a surge of insulin secretion to clear excess glucose (blood sugar) from the blood. Insulin also clears a large amount of the LNAAs from the blood, sending them into muscle cells. Yet the carbohydrate-released insulin has little effect on tryptophan, allowing most of it to remain in the blood and raising the tryptophan ratio. Over the past 25 years Dr. Richard Wurtman of MIT and his neuroscientist wife Dr. Judith Wurtman have presented much evidence to show that many people suffering from a host of disorders—ranging from SAD (seasonal/sunlight affective disorder) and PMS (premenstrual syndrome) to eating disorders such as carbohydrate-craving obesity and bulimia—may be instinctively utilizing the high carbohydrate strategy to elevate their brain serotonin production. One major drawback of this approach is that insulin not only increases brain serotonin production—it also "instructs" fat cells to convert the fats, sugars and aminos that insulin clears from the blood into stored body fat!

Even after trypotophan enters the brain, there are still more potential roadblocks on the path to serotonin production. Once tryptophan enters serotonin nerve cells, it is converted by a two-step process into serotonin. In the first step, tryptophan is converted into 5-HTP by an enzyme called "tryptophan hydroxylase." This enzyme requires adequate oxygen, a sulfhydryl factor (a molecule containing sulfur), and a folic acid-derived "reduced pteridine factor" to function normally. Folic acid, a B-vitamin, is found most plentifully in dark green leafy vegetables and organ meats—hardly a mainstay of the American diet—and may be destroyed by cooking, light exposure and stomach acid. Dr. Simon Young, one of the major serotonin researchers of the past 20 years, discussed the evidence linking folic acid deficiency to sereotonin deficiency in his 1989 Borden Award lecture.[2] He concluded unequivocally, based on both human and animal studies, that folic acid deficiency does promote inadequate brain serotonin production in some people, leading to depression and other psychological disorders.

Another difficulty in the conversion of tryptophan to 5-HTP by the enzyme tryptophan hydroxylase (TH) was also noted by Young. Under normal conditions, TH is only 50 percent saturated. This means that much of the enzyme is lying idle, like a factory producing at only 50 percent of capacity. The TH-mediated tryptophan-5-HTP conversion is thus said to be the "rate-limiting" step in serotonin production. Unless higher-than-normal amounts of tryptophan are supplied to the TH enzymes inside serotonin neurons, serotonin production will not increase. And because of the tryptophan-LNAA competition for entry into the brain, it is not easy to increase tryptophan supplies for the TH to work on.

Once 5-HTP has been formed, it is quickly converted into serotonin. The enzyme that converts 5-HTP to serotonin is a vitamin B6-activated enzyme called "L-Aromatic Amino Acid Decarboxylase" (LAAD). LAAD is normally not considered a problem in serotonin production, since it so rapidly converts its substrate (the molecule it works on) (5-HTP) to serotonin. Yet, in a 1995 paper Dr. P. Hartvig and colleagues reported evidence that vitamin B6 supplementation could increase brain levels of serotonin in both rats and monkeys.[3] Using radioactively-labeled 5-HTP and PET-scan technology (a type of imaging of body tissues), the Hartvig group found that intravenously administering vitamin B6 to Rhesus monkeys increased their conversion of 5-HTP to serotonin at an average rate of about 20 percent. A 1990 study by Drs. A. K. Kant and G. Block found dietary B6 intake in the U.S. population low even by RDA standards.[4] Thus, the 5-HTP-serotonin conversion cannot be assumed to always proceed optimally.

In the 1970s the American health food industry provided an alternative method for getting tryptophan to the brain—tryptophan supplements. Many people found that 500–3,000 mg of supplementary tryptophan provided relief from such serotonin-related problems as depression, insomnia and PMS. In 1989 the FDA removed tryptophan from the U.S. market due to a serious ailment—eosinophilia myalgia—caused by a single batch of contaminated tryptophan from a single Japanese producer.[5] Although the problem was with this manufacturer only, the FDA has still not allowed tryptophan back on the market as of 1998, and shows no signs of doing so any time soon. It is available, however, in other countries around the world.

In Europe, an alternative to tryptophan has been available for over 20 years—the intermediary between tryptophan and serotonin, 5-HTP. Europeans have pioneered the use of 5-HTP in human clinical research since the 1960s. In some ways supplemental 5-HTP has acted like a "better tryptophan," while in other ways it has been shown to act differently than supplemental tryptophan.

TRYPTOPHAN VS 5-HTP—WHAT'S THE DIFFERENCE?

Research since the 1960s has discovered many differences between tryptophan and 5-HTP supplements.

1) Tryptophan is needed in many metabolic pathways besides those for serotonin production, while 5-HTP is only known to have one use in the body—serotonin production.

2) Tryptophan is degraded by the liver enzyme tryptophan pyrrolase; 5-HTP does not suffer this fate. The level of liver pyrrolase activity is determined by the availability of tryptophan. Thus increasing tryptophan intake induces higher pyrrolase activity, in effect destroying much tryptophan before it can even reach the general blood circulation.

3) Tryptophan travels through the bloodstream mostly bound to the blood protein albumin—only 5 percent may travel as free tryptophan. Yet, 5-HTP is transported through the bloodstream almost completely albumin-unbound. Thus as Dr. Zmilacher and coworkers noted "L-5-HTP easily crosses the blood-brain barrier since most L-5-HTP in plasma is not bound to albumin."[6]

(The "L" in front of 5-HTP refers to the chemical structure of the molecule.)

4) The **ratio** of tryptophan to other LNAAs in the bloodstream may be the crucial determinant in how much tryptophan enters the brain. There is no reported evidence that 5-HTP entry into the brain is affected by the LNAAs.

5) Tryptophan and 5-HTP have both been used in many human clinical studies. The dosages of tryptophan used have ranged from 1,000–9,000 mg, with 3,000–9,000 mg being most common. Human clinical studies typically use 150–900 mg 5-HTP, and most have used 300 mg or less. Thus 5-HTP seems to be 10–20 times more potent than tryptophan.

6) At high doses (6,000–10,000 mg) tryptophan may "overcompete" with tyrosine and reduce its entry into the brain. Production of the important neurotransmitters dopamine and norandrenalin may then decrease. And while serotonin is an important antidepressant neurotransmitter, so are dopamine and noradrenalin. High doses of tryptophan have generally been found less successful in human depression studies than lower doses, possibly due to diminished brain tyrosine transport.[7] Depression studies done with 5-HTP have frequently found evidence that 5-HTP actually increases brain dopamine and noradrenalin activity, through a currently unknown mechanism.

5-HTP VS. SEROTONIN-ENHANCING DRUGS

Since the 1950s, various types of drugs have been used by doctors and psychiatrists to enhance brain monoamine neurotransmitter function. The first medical antidepressant was iproniazid, a monoamine oxidase inhibitor (MAOI). Monoamine oxidase (MAO) is an enzyme present inside neurons, where it serves to break down monoamine (MA) neurotransmitters such as serotonin. Some MA neurotransmitters are broken down as soon as they're formed, even before they can be released into the synaptic gap to "fire" the next neuron. MAs such as serotonin which do cross the synaptic gap are sooner or later taken back by the neuron that secreted them. They are then either repackaged for reuse, or destroyed by MAO enzymes. MAOI drugs thus act to increase the availability of serotonin and other MAs by preventing their breakdown by

MAO enzymes. This may increase the intraneuronal levels of serotonin and other MAs by 300 percent.[8] However, MAOIs can also increase the neuronal levels of another substance called "tyramine" to dangerously high levels, possibly resulting in stroke, unless a special low-tyramine diet is rigidly followed by those who take MAOI drugs. Hence MAOIs have proven too dangerous for widespread use to enhance brain serotonin levels.

The next generation of drugs believed to enhance brain serotonin and noradrenalin became available in the 1960s: the tricyclic antidepressant (TCA) drugs, such as imipramine and amitriptyline. TCAs seem to attach to and inhibit the neuronal reuptake sites for serotonin, preventing the return of serotonin molecules to the neuron which secreted them. This enhances serotonin action in two ways. Since most serotonin returned to its source neuron is broken down by MAO enzymes, TCAs slow serotonin catabolism (breakdown). TCAs also cause more serotonin to remain in the synaptic gap. This increases the frequency with which serotonin molecules connect with their receptors on the postsynaptic (receiving) neuron, which in turn increases serotonin neurotransmission. However, TCAs also affect other receptors on neurons which respond to acetylcholine, histamine, dopamine and noradrenalin. Users of TCAs thus suffer from a wide range of unpleasant side effects, ranging from drowsiness, confusion, and blurred vision to hypotension (low blood pressure) and movement disorders.[9] TCAs are now considered "antiquated" by psychiatrists, although some general practice physicians still favor them.

The latest round of serotonin drugs are the serotonin-specific reuptake inhibitors (SSRIs). The first and most famous of these is fluoxetine, more popularly known as Prozac®. Other SSRIs such as paroxetine (Paxil®), sertraline (Zoloft®) and fluvoxamine (Luvox®) are also now in vogue in America and Europe. These drugs are used to treat eating disorders and obsessive-compulsive disorders as well as depression. They have put serotonin "on the map" as the "mood molecule" in the public eye. Serotonin drugs were the cover story for *Time* magazine, September 29, 1997. The article was prompted by the September 1997 withdrawal from the U.S. market of two "superstar" serotonin-enhancing drugs—fenfluramine (Pondimin®) and dexfenfluramine (Redux®). Chemically related to Prozac, these two drugs had been widely used in America and Europe to treat obesity and promote weight loss even in the merely "plump." They both work by stimulating release of serotonin from neurons, as well as by inhibiting serotonin reuptake. Studies on monkeys had hinted for years at possible brain damage from these drugs. When it was discovered in 1997 that as many as 30 percent of even brief users of the drugs might develop possibly life-threatening heart valve damage, the FDA and the manufacturers hastily recalled them from the market. The *Time* article noted that "so far, the [drug] tools used to manipulate serotonin in the brain are more like machetes than they are like scalpels—crudely effective but capable of doing plenty of collateral damage." Dr. Robert Julien, in his text *A Primer of Drug Action,* notes that side effects of Prozac may include nervousness, anxiety, sexual dysfunction, insomnia, nausea, loss of appetite, motor restlessness and muscle rigidity. He also notes that when used to treat panic disorder, Prozac may even worsen the attacks or lead to mania.[9] Thus for those in need of a boost for their brain serotonin activity, the serotonin-enhancing medical drugs all suffer from an excessive "risk-benefit ratio"—the risks outweigh the rewards.

SAFETY AND SIDE EFFECTS

5-HTP has been used in clinical studies for over 30 years, and has been in medical use in Europe for over 20 years. 5-HTP first entered the American market in 1990 after the tryptophan ban, and by 1997 was widely available at health food stores and from mail-order vitamin companies. 5-HTP is a molecule as natural to the brain as is water or glucose—or serotonin. No serotonin drug can make that claim: they are all "xenobiotics"—foreign molecules, alien to the body and to normal brain metabolism. And, unlike the serotonin drugs, 5-HTP has compiled an excellent safety record through years of clinical study and ever-increasing public use. Thus a 1987 review of past clinical 5-HTP studies by Dr. W. F. Byerley and coworkers (see page 40) concluded that "oral administration of 5-HTP . . . is associated with few adverse effects." In a 1991 paper reporting the results of a major study comparing 5-HTP to the SSRI fluvoxamine in the treatment of depression, Dr. W. Pöldinger and colleagues note that, "in general, 5-HTP-induced adverse events worthy of note are rare within the therapeutic dose range."[10] Dr. C. Cangiano and his group conclude their 1992 report on the use of 5-HTP in treating obesity with the statement that "the good tolerance to 5-HTP treatment observed suggest that this substance may be safely used in the long-term treatment of obesity."[11] One of the most enthusiastic proponents of 5-HTP use for depression, Dr. L. J. van Hiele, reported in 1980 that, "we found no contraindications or significant side effects in our series; nor did we find any mention of them in the literature. Follow-ups of the blood pressure, liver function and urine, and EEG's, revealed no anomalies."[12] When compared to the many varieties of serotonin drugs, it is obvious that 5-HTP wins the safety test comparison easily.

Despite its 30-plus years of successful clinical testing and use, 5-HTP does occasionally trigger unwanted and unpleasant side effects, primarily in the gastrointestinal tract. The enzyme LAAD, which converts 5-HTP to serotonin, is found in areas outside the brain. Liver, kidneys, stomach and small intestine all contain relatively high levels of LAAD, and will thus convert some ingested 5-HTP to serotonin.

In the stomach and intestine, serotonin promotes muscle contraction and plays an essential role in normal intestinal peristalsis (wavelike motion) and digestion. However, excessively high stomach or intestinal levels of serotonin may provoke unpleasant reactions—nausea, cramping, diarrhea, even vomiting.

Over the history of 5-HTP studies, occasional gastrointestinal upset has been the main reported side effect from 5-HTP use, due to intestinal serotonin formation from 5-HTP. Most researchers have found that only a small portion of 5-HTP users experience these side effects. They are usually transitory, diminishing or disappearing with continued use. They are more likely to occur with high starting doses of 5-HTP, or when doses are raised quickly.

Some researchers, such as Drs. H. M van Praag[13] and Pöldinger,[10] have reported that taking 5-HTP with meals virtually eliminates the gastric side effects. In the 1991 Pöldinger study, only 1 of 36 patients receiving 5-HTP dropped out of the study because of adverse intestinal reactions, while 3 of 33 fluvoxamine (SSRI) patients dropped out due to intestinal side effects. Nonetheless, those suffering from gut disorders such as ulcers, irritable bowl syndrome, Crohn's disease, celiac disease (sprue), etc., and those with just an extremely "sensitive" GI tract, should probably use 5-HTP with great caution or not at all.

5-HTP AND ACUTE TRYPTOPHAN DEPLETION

In the last decade a new method of studying brain serotonin activity has been widely used in both animals and humans—acute tryptophan depletion (ATD). ATD is a method used to rapidly and powerfully deplete brain serotonin levels through rapid lowering of blood tryptophan levels. In lab animals, ATD has been shown to alter many serotonin-linked behaviors: ATD increases pain sensitivity, increases the startle response to loud noises, reduces rapid eye movement (REM) sleep, and increases aggression in rats undergoing ATD. These behavioral expressions of experimentally produced brain serotonin depletion are rapidly reversed when blood tryptophan levels are once again increased, allowing new brain serotonin synthesis. A reduction in the plasma (blood) tryptophan level of 80 percent can be accomplished in humans in three to five hours by administering a tryptophan-free amino acid drink. The tryptophan-free amino acid drink induces liver protein synthesis and thereby depletes available plasma tryptophan, as it is "stolen" by the liver to use in the induced protein synthesis.

When ATD was used with healthy male subjects, it produced a mild impairment in attention-demanding tasks while increasing subjective reports of negative mood, without producing full-blown depression. Delgado and coworkers used ATD to study the effects of lowering plasma and brain tryptophan levels, and thus brain serotonin levels, on 21 depressed patients who were in remission through serotonin-enhancing drug treatment.[14] Their experiment was a double-blind, placebo controlled, crossover study, so that eventually all 21 patients experienced both the control high-tryptophan amino acid drink and the experimental tryptophan-free high dose amino acid drink. "Crossover" means that the groups alternated as to the treatment (placebo or the drink) they received. A modified version of the standard Hamilton Depression Rating Scale (a psychological test) was used to measure their depression levels before and after the control and experimental ATD treatments. The control testing produced no significant change in depression scores. However, ATD rapidly evoked such core depressive symptoms as depressed mood, insomnia, decreased appetite, loss of energy, interest and pleasure, decreased concentration and a sense of worthlessness and failure in 14 of the 21 remitted depressed patients. The ATD treatment reduced plasma tryptophan levels up to 90 percent within five hours. In lab animals this degree of plasma tryptophan depletion reduces brain levels of serotonin 60–70 percent in a similar time period. In-vitro (test tube) studies show that serotonin neurons will use up available serotonin stores in one to two hours after tryptophan depletion. The degree of plasma tryptophan depletion was strongly correlated with the Hamilton depression scores obtained seven hours after the tryptophan-free amino acid drink was given. The study authors also commented on how closely the symptoms induced by ATD resembled the unique clinical features manifested by each patient before their successful drug treatment for depression. Depression symptoms disappeared within 24 to 48 hours after resumption of meals with normal tryptophan content. All three antidepressant drug types—MAOIs, TCAs, and SSRIs—were represented among the 14 patients experiencing serious depressive relapse due to ATD.[14]

The lesson to be learned from the ATD experiment is very simple. The successful clinical action of serotonin-enhancing drugs is dependent upon some unknown minimum level of serotonin being produced by serotonin neurons. The various types of serotonin drugs merely work by amplifying the effect of **existing** serotonin stores within serotonin neurons. All serotonin within neurons is produced within them directly from 5-HTP. And neuronal 5-HTP comes either from tryptophan or 5-HTP supplements delivered to brain cells from the bloodstream. Which, therefore, would seem to be the more logical and natural method of increasing brain serotonin activity—the natural precursor of serotonin, 5-HTP, or xenobiotic (foreign to the body), potentially toxic drugs whose activity depends upon 5-HTP in any case?

5-HTP AND DRUG INTERACTIONS

Given that serotonin-potentiating drugs are biochemically dependent for their success on neuronal 5-HTP/serotonin levels, it is not surprising that a few human clinical trials have used a combination of 5-HTP and an antidepressant drug. In 1976, Lopez-Ibor and coworkers reported successful results combining 50–300 mg 5-HTP/day with an MAOI—nialamide.[15] Twelve of 15 patients given the combination "markedly" improved. The combination-treated patients also had a "fuller and faster" recovery from depression than the control group, which received nialamide only. In 1980, Mendelwicz and Youdin reported the results of a study comparing placebo, 5-HTP alone and 5-HTP plus deprenyl, a nontoxic MAOI.[16] They found the 5-HTP plus deprenyl combination superior to 5-HTP alone for treating depression. And van Praag (1974) found the combination of clomipramine and 5-HTP superior to 5-HTP alone in treating therapy-resistant depression.[17] Van Praag used a low dose of clomipramine in his small study, thus indicating the power of 5-HTP to amplify the effect of serotonin-enhancing drugs. Yet these few indications of possible 5-HTP-serotonin drug synergy should be interpreted with caution, due to the possibility of a clinically-induced toxic phenomenon—the "serotonin syndrome."

THE SEROTONIN SYNDROME

In 1991, Harvey Sternbach, M.D. reported results of a review of published scientific literature on the "serotonin syndrome" in humans and animals.[18] Sternbach reviewed 12 reports of 38 cases in human patients conducted between 1982 and 1990. The serotonin syndrome is a condition of overstimulation and overactivity of serotonin neural circuits, especially in the brain stem and spinal cord. It is a result of combining tryptopohan or 5-HTP with prescription drugs. The symptoms in humans involved mental changes such as confusion, hypomania (a mild form of mania), agitation and "feeling drunk," as well as extreme restlessness, muscle twitches, hyperreactive (overreactive) reflexes, intense sweating, shivering, tremor, diarrhea, fever and incoordination. In some cases the syndrome led to coma and death. The syndrome did not occur spontaneously or naturally, but was caused by the various drug interactions. The most common combination to trigger the syndrome was an MAOI combined either with tryptophan or fluoxetine (Prozac). Tryptophan combined with only fluoxetine also caused some cases, as did clomipramine plus an MAOI. Treatment of the syndrome was based on the specific symptoms of the patients, but also required discontinuation of the drug combinations. Once treatment and discontinuance was begun, the syndrome typically resolved in 24 hours, although confusion might last for days. In a few cases, death ensued even with prompt and heroic medical care. Sternbach also points out that the medical community's awareness of the serotonin syndrome is less than optimal, leading to both inappropriate drug combinations which may provoke the syndrome, as well as possible failure to diagnose and treat the syndrome when it presents at doctors' offices or emergency rooms. Sternbach also believes the syndrome to be underreported by physicians, due to lack of awareness. Given that many of the cases Sternback examined involved tryptopohan along with a serotonin drug, and given that 5-HTP is even more potent than tryptophan as a brain serotonin booster, both physicians and patients should use extreme care in combining 5-HTP with MAOIs or SSRIs.

5-HTP VS. DEPRESSION: CASE STUDIES

By far the greatest number of human clinical studies using 5-HTP have focused on its use as a natural antidepressant. "Depression" in the medical sense of the term refers to more than just a sad or down mood. Depression is considered a syndrome—that is, a cluster of symptoms. Besides looking at the quality of mood when diagnosing depression, clinicians will also consider a patient's "vegetative" features—sleep, appetite, weight changes and sex drive; cognitive features such as memory, attention span and frustration tolerance; impulse control issues, such as suicide attempts or impulsive violence; behavioral features such as motivation, pleasure, loss of interest in normal activities; and physical features such as headaches, muscle tension and intestinal disorders. Psychiatrists subdivide depression into various types. Major depression, also called vital, endogenous, or melancholic depression is the most serious variety. Dysthymic depression, sometimes called neurotic or personal depression, is a more "low grade" depression, although often more chronic as well. A distinction is also made between unipolar depression, which involves only depressive swings from "normalcy," and bipolar depression, also called manic-depression, where the patient oscillates between depressive and euphoric, hyperactive, delusional, grandiose mental-behavioral states.[19] It is estimated that 20–25 percent of all women will experience at least one major depressive episode in their lives, while only 8–12 percent of men are likely to experience major depression.[20] About 10–15 million Americans are estimated to be depressed in any given year. An estimated 30,000 suicides per year are linked to depression, and a huge toll in lost jobs, wrecked marriages, drug/alcohol abuse, accidents and violence are also part of the costs of depression.[19]

In the 1950s it was discovered that certain medical drugs such as reserpine could induce depression while simultaneously lowering the monoamine (MA) neurotransmitter level in the brain. This information, combined with the discovery that the original antidepressant drugs—the MAOIs and TCAs—seemed to work through raising MA levels in the brain, led scientists to propose the MA theory of depression. The MA theory holds that for various reasons (stress, diet, drug abuse, genetics, etc.) a depressed person's brain develops low levels of certain classes of neurotransmitters—either the catecholamine MAs (dopamine and noradrenalin) or the indoleamine MA (serotonin) or both. The low brain MA levels then disrupt normal brain function, leading to depression. By the 1960s and 1970s, European research focused mainly on serotonin. Depression runs in families—a family history of depression increases a person's risk of depression as much as 300 percent, thus suggesting a genetic component to depression. And by the early 1970s it was known that dietary habits could easily influence brain serotonin biochemistry adversely. These observations, combined with the original antidepressant drugs' tendencies to raise brain serotonin levels, led clinicians to try serotonin precursors—tryptophan and 5-HTP—in the treatment of depression. The results with tryptophan were inconclusive—a 1981 review by van Praag noted that only five of ten double-blind depression studies using tryptophan found it to be effective.[21] In a double-blind test, neither the experimenter nor the test subjects know who is getting the "real stuff" (5-HTP, in this case), and who is getting a placebo. A placebo is a "dummy pill" (or injection or other substance) that looks just like the capsule or tablet containing the experimental substance, but is an inert (unreactive) substance. In medical and psychiatric studies, 15–35 percent of people tested will respond successfully to a placebo, getting better or even "cured." This effect presumably represents the (possibly unconscious) power of faith or belief in medical treatment to produce positive results. Patients are assigned randomly to the placebo or test ingredient group, and a neutral third party keeps records of who got the placebo and who got the test substance. When a clinical trial is concluded, the results of patients receiving the active test ingredient are compared to the results from those getting the placebo. Only if there is a statistically significant positive difference between the results achieved with the test substance vs. the results gotten with the placebo is the trial considered a successful validation of the experimental therapy. A 1982 study by Thompson and coworkers, however, found tryptophan to be as effective as the

TCA amitriptyline in a group of 150 mild to moderately depressed outpatients.[22]

Human depression studies with 5-HTP began by the 1960s. A 1967 *Lancet* report by Drs. T. Persson and B. E. Roos related their success with 5-HTP in a therapy-resistant patient.[23] By 1972, Dr. I. Sano of Japan reported results of an open trial (non-placebo controlled) using 50–300 mg 5-HTP/day with 107 endogenous (major) depressed patients, for a period of one to five weeks.[24] Both unipolar and bipolar types of depression were represented in his study. Of the patients, 74 (69 percent) were reported as either "cured" or showing "marked improvement." The first double-blind placebo-controlled test of 5-HTP for depression was also reported in 1972 by Dr. H. M. van Praag.[25] Although his patient sample was small (ten) and the success modest, van Praag claimed his study validated 5-HTP treatment. His patients were all selected on a basis of severe unremitting depression, refractory (resistant) to treatment. Three of the five patients on 5-HTP improved, while none of the placebo patients got better—indeed, two got worse. And when a placebo was secretly substituted for the 5-HTP in the three patients who got better, two of them promptly relapsed, thus further indicating the antidepressant effect of 5-HTP.

5-HTP AND THE PROBENECID TEST

Dr. H. M. van Praag is a Dutch psychiatrist who has focused on tryptophan, 5-HTP and serotonin biology in depression and other psychobiologic disorders. He has produced more papers, books and book chapters on 5-HTP/serotonin studies and issues than any other researcher. We have already mentioned his work several times in this guide. He has pioneered many of the key concepts and methods of understanding and treating serotonin deficiency-related depression. His 1972 5-HTP study, was not only the first published double-blind 5-HTP study it was also a pilot study to examine the predictive value of the probenecid test, given to determine who is likely to benefit from 5-HTP therapy in depression.

Throughout the 1960s, '70s, and '80s many reports were published which examined the cerebral spinal fluid (CSF) levels of serotonin's chief metabolite (breakdown product)—5-hydroxyindoleacetic acid (5-HIAA)—in depression, and also how these levels differed from healthy control subjects' CSF 5-HIAA levels. When the MAO enzymes inside serotonin neurons "digest" serotonin, they convert it into a waste product—5-HIAA—that is then secreted into the CSF, which bathes the brain and fills the spinal cord. The 5-HIAA slowly travels down the spinal cord fluid, and even more slowly diffuses into the bloodstream. Because 5-HIAA is normally leaked by the brain into the CSF more quickly than it leaks from CSF into the blood, there is a net accumulation of 5-HIAA at the base of the spine. Doctors can remove a small sample of this lumbar (lower spine) CSF with a needle and then measure its 5-HIAA content. As Paul Willner notes in his massive review work *Depression—A Psychobiological Synthesis*, "Measurement of lumbar CSF therefore provides a reasonable estimate of brain 5-HTP [serotonin] turnover . . ."[26] Since serotonin deficiency depressions are believed to result from reduced serotonin metabolism (turnover) and neurotransmission, this should be reflected in

lower CSF 5-HIAA levels in depressed patients compared to non-depressed healthy test subjects. As Willner notes, most but not all studies have shown this correlation.

A further refinement on the CSF 5-HIAA test as a marker for serotonin-related depression was developed by van Praag and several other researchers independently.[25] When a harmless substance called "probenecid" was given (partly intravenously, partly orally) to test subjects, it significantly raised the amount of 5-HIAA that accumulated in CSF in a given period of time. Probenecid accomplishes this by preventing the CSF 5-HIAA from leaking into the bloodstream. This amplifies or highlights the differences between 5-HIAA levels in depressed and nondepressed people. In a probenecid test, baseline (initial) lumbar CSF levels of 5-HIAA are taken at 9 A.M. Two days later probenecid is administered over a four-hour period, and a second lumbar CSF sample is taken eight hours after the first probenecid dose. In van Praag's control group (depressed patients), the increase in CSF 5-HIAA after probenecid averaged 313 percent, with a range of 131–729 percent. In the three patients from this group who responded well to 5-HTP, the probenecid test increased their CSF 5-HIAA levels only slightly, indicating that these patients weren't metabolizing serotonin. (The test was done before the start of 5-HTP treatment.) In the two patients who were 5-HTP nonresponders, post-probenecid 5-HIAA increased to a greater extent, indicating their serotonin levels were normal. The placebo group averaged in the low to normal range. Van Praag thus concluded that probenecid testing was a useful method to differentiate low-serotonin depressives from "normoserotonergic" depressives (those with normal levels of serotonin). Since 5-HTP acts primarily through conversion to serotonin, it was hardly surprising that 5-HTP would be most likely to help those suffering from slow serotonin metabolism/neurotransmission, as evidenced by their low baseline or post-probenecid levels of CSF 5-HIAA. Willner noted that two thirds of the post-probenecid studies found evidence of reduced CSF 5-HIAA in depressives, compared to controls. These findings provide empirical (scientific) support to the theory that some depressions are linked to low-brain serotonin metabolism/neurotransmission, and that 5-HTP, as the immediate precursor of serotonin, is a natural and rational approach to treating such "serotonin-deficiency" depressions.

Japanese neuropsychiatrist M. Kaneko and colleagues provided a different kind of evidence on 5-HTP use in 1979.[27] They gave 18 young and middle-aged depressed Japanese patients 150 or 300 mg of 5-HTP for 10–28 days. They found two patients to be very much improved and eight to be much improved. They thus considered 5-HTP a success in 10 of 18 or 55 percent of their patients. The Kaneko group also ran blood tests on their patients to determine blood serotonin levels before and after treatment. Also, 47 healthy control subjects were tested for their baseline serotonin blood levels. The blood serotonin levels of the control group averaged 150 ng/ml (ng=nanograms). In the nine 5-HTP-responders treated, blood serotonin levels went from 78 to 148 ng/ml after treatment, a statistically significant increase to a level almost identical to the healthy controls. In the three nonresponders whose blood was tested, serotonin levels rose from 56 to 77 ng/ml, a nonsignificant increase to a level only half that of both the control group and the 5-HTP-responders. Kaneko thus concluded that in some depressed patients "there is some sort of reduction of the absorption of L-5-HTP in the gastrointestinal tract and of the decarboxylation [metabolism] to serotonin." Other studies focusing on 5-HTP intestinal absorption have also found evidence of variable absorption of 5-HTP among different people, thus possibly explaining the occasional negative results found with 5-HTP in depression studies.[28,29]

In 1991, H. Agren and coworkers published results of a positron emission tomography (PET) imaging test using radioactively-labelled 5-HTP in eight healthy volunteers and six depressed patients.[30] Some of the depressed patients were tested both while depressed and again months later when in remission due to treatment. After patients and controls were intravenously infused with (slightly) radioactive 5-HTP, a PET camera took "pictures" of certain brain regions for 40 minutes, measuring the gradual accumulation of 5-HTP in brain cells. Graphs of 5-HTP accumulation in both the whole brain and a specific brain region (the basal ganglia) were prepared from the data for both controls and patients. There was a statistically significant difference in 5-HTP accumulation between controls and depressed patients in both whole brain and basal ganglia, averaging 30 percent less in the depressed patients. Two of the depressed patients were retested months later when in remission and produced 5-HTP accumulation data almost identical to their active depression levels. The researchers concluded that "our results indicate a distinctly lower uptake of the serotonin precursor 5-HTP across the blood-brain barrier in depression compared with healthy individuals." Taken together, the acute trypto-phan depletion studies cited earlier, CSF 5-HIAA tests (both baseline and post-probenecid), absorption studies, blood serotonin studies and PET brain-scan 5-HTP study all indicate significant abnormalities (compared to nondepressed people) of tryptophan, 5-HTP and serotonin metabolism/neurotransmission in a significant number of depressed people.

TO PDI OR NOT TO PDI?

The approach taken for the use of 5-HTP in the Sano[24] and Kaneko[27] studies cited earlier contrasts to the method of 5-HTP use favored by van Praag and other researchers that he has influenced. Van Praag and these others such as van Hiele,[12] have suggested that 5-HTP always be combined with a peripheral decarboxylase inhibitor (PDI). However, many researchers including Sano have employed 5-HTP without using a PDI, as did the most impressive 5-HTP/depression trial yet reported the Pöldinger study.[10]

The enzyme L-aromatic amino acid decarboxylase (LAAD), which converts 5-HTP to serotonin, is found outside the brain, and is especially plentiful in some liver, kidney, stomach and intestinal lining cells. When this noncerebral LAAD converts 5-HTP to serotonin, it may cause intestinal distress, reduced 5-HTP absorption, and reduced levels of 5-HTP for brain serotonin synthesis. PDIs are synthetic drugs (carbidopa and benserazide are the most commonly used) which will inhibit LAAD and minimize conversion of 5-HTP to serotonin outside the brain. PDIs will not, however, penetrate the blood-brain barrier and inhibit brain serotonin synthesis at normally used dosages. At first glance, combining PDIs with 5-HTP to enhance brain serotonin synthesis would seem to be the best course of action. Yet a review of the 5-HTP-depression literature casts significant doubt on the benefit of combined PDI use. In 1988, Dr. K. Zmilacher and associates published the results of a small study using 5-HTP with PDI in 13 depressed patients and 5-HTP without PDI in 13 patients.[6] Their patients were a very therapy-resistant group, averaging five previous depressive episodes and an 8–25-year-long duration of illness. Many of them remained on various psychiatric drugs during the 5-HTP trial. Eleven were classified as having "severe" depressions, 15 as "marked" depressions, with more severe depression patients in the 5-HTP-only group. Average 5-HTP treatment length was six to eight weeks, with 5-HTP doses starting at 100 mg per day and working up to 300 mg if needed. The 5-HTP treatment was assessed as showing "very good" or "good" results in 7 of the 13 patients, while the 5-HTP plus PDI group yielded 6 of 12 "very good" or "good" results. While some critics might consider the combined treatment efficacy of the two 5-HTP groups—52 percent—as somewhat modest, the Zmilacher group stated that given the long illness duration, frequent relapse rate, and resistance to standard therapy in their patient group, the results were actually rather good. They found no statistically significant difference in treatment efficacy between the 5-HTP alone vs. 5-HTP/PDI groups. However, a rather obvious difference in side effects was noted between the two groups. The 5-HTP-only group had five people report 9 side effects, mostly intestinal upset, while the 5-HTP/PDI group had six patients report 19 side effects. These included various emotional (anxiety) and bodily (blurred vision and fatigue) symptoms that did not occur in the 5-HTP-only group. The 5-HTP-only group also required a lower 5-HTP dose (average 192 mg) than the 5-HTP/PDI group (average 231 mg), even though the 5-HTP-only group contained seven "severe" depressions, with only four "severe" cases in the PDI group. Zmilacher and coworkers concluded that "there was no evidence that benserazide [the PDI] intensified the efficacy of L-5-HTP. A review of [17 studies] on this subject revealed that L-5-HTP given alone was more effective (249 out of 389 patients, 64 percent) than the combination of L-5-HTP with a [PDI] (93 out of 176 patients, 52.9 percent)." Thus, given the record of 5-HTP with and without PDIs, and given that PDIs are prescription drugs that may induce side effects, while 5-HTP is a food supplement that occurs naturally in the body, PDI use with 5-HTP must be considered unnecessary and possibly even counterproductive.

SEROTONIN DEFICIENCY IN DEPRESSION: CAUSE OR SUSCEPTIBILITY FACTOR?

In 1980 van Praag and de Haan reported the results of a different kind of 5-HTP-depression study.[31] Based on a survey of the literature, van Praag had concluded that brain serotonin deficiency might more properly be considered a predisposing or susceptibility factor in depression rather than a direct cause of depression. He also noted that the abnormal CSF 5-HIAA results usually continued in patients successfully treated for depression with 5-HTP both during and after treatment, suggesting persistent serotonin abnormalities. Van Praag and de Haan therefore set up a long-term study with 13 women and seven men suffering from recurrent major depression. During the four years before the study began, all 20 had each been hospitalized three or more times due to depressive episodes. Fourteen patients were unipolar (depressive swings from normalcy); while six were bipolar (manic-depressive) patients. In 13 patients a subnormal post-probenecid 5-HIAA level was observed, both during depressive periods and during asymtomatic intervals. The average level of 5-HIAA in the group at most recent testing was 47 ng/ml. In the other seven patients 5-HIAA was always within (low) normal limits, with the most recent group average being 119ng/ml. The patients were randomly divided into two groups of ten. For a period of one year, group A received 200 mg 5-HTP plus 150 mg carbidopa (a PDI) daily, with the dose being slowly increased to that level from the beginning. During the second year they received identically appearing placebo capsules. In group B, the 5-HTP/placebo sequence was reversed. Patients were seen at least once every four weeks, at which time their mental status was evaluated. The Hamilton Depression Rating Scale was used, and a three-point global rating scale was related to mood, motor activity and ability to experience emotions. Patients' blood pressure, blood picture, liver and kidney functions were also tested. A score of two or higher on the global rating scale and/or a score of 21 or more on the Hamilton Scale was defined as a relapse. In that case the patient would be treated with the TCA clomipramine, with 5-HTP, or the placebo would be continued. The clomipramine would be withdrawn four weeks after disappearance of the depressive symptoms.

During the placebo year, group A had nine patients develop one or more relapse, with a group total of fourteen relapses; group B had eight patients develop one or more relapse for a group total of ten relapses. During the 5-HTP period group A had three patients with one relapse each for a group total of 3, while group B had three patients with one or more relapses for a group total of 4. Combining the two groups, 17 of 20 patients developed 24 relapses during their placebo years, an average rate of 1.2 relapses per patient per year. The combined 5-HTP groups had 6 of 20 patients experience 7 relapses, a rate of 0.35 relapses per patient per year. Statistical tests indicated that there was only a 0.1 percent probability that the results were due to random chance.

The average depression score for both groups while on placebo or 5-HTP also clearly indicated the difference between the groups. On the 0–3 depression scale both 5-HTP groups averaged between 0–1 episodes each month (for most months 0–0.5), while the placebo groups averaged 1.5–2.3 most months. This indicated much more severe depressive symptomatology overall when the patients did not receive 5-HTP.

The post-probenecid 5-HIAA status of the patients also revealed clear-cut differences. Five of seven patients with persistently normal post-probenecid 5-HIAA levels relapsed while taking 5-HTP, while only 1 of 13 patients with persistently subnormal post-probenecid 5-HIAA relapsed on 5-HTP. Van Praag and de Haan[31] conclude their study (after also discussing other relevant data from the 5-HTP/serotonin literature) with the statement that: "The data presented support the hypothesis that (1) central brain serotonergic [activated by or capable of liberating serotonin] systems are involved in mood regulations; (2) these systems are permanently disturbed in a certain category of depressive patients; (3) this leads to depression 'vulnerability'—an increased tendency to respond to [noxious] stimuli with . . . depression of mood; (4) increased vulnerability to depression can be reduced with the aid of 5-HTP."

One of the more impressive studies with 5-HTP in depression

was reported by Dutch psychiatrist L. J. van Hiele in 1980.[12] Van Hiele used 5-HTP in a wide range of doses (50–600 mg, average dose 200 mg) combined with a PDI to treat 99 therapy-resistant depression patients. Forty-three of his patients recovered completely on 5-HTP, while eight showed "evident improvement," for a success rate of 51 percent. Since standard antidepressant drugs are typically claimed to have a 60–70 percent "cure" rate in depression, van Hiele's results at first glance don't seem that impressive. Yet van Hiele's group of patients were all "hard to cure" depressives. The length of their depressions was well beyond the average (which is 6–24 months), ranging from seven to ten years. The patients had also typically been treated without success by standard antidepressants for an average of 18–24 months by van Hiele before he began their 5-HTP therapy. For 17 of his 5-HTP successes, it was the third antidepressant tried, while for 30 of his successes, 5-HTP was the fourth, fifth or sixth therapy tried. Thus van Hiele notes that the risk of a significant placebo effect in his study was low. Many of his patients were able to discontinue or lower the dose of their (previously unsuccessful) multiple antidepressant medications. Thirty-two of the 51 successful 5-HTP cases did still require some dose of imipramine, a TCA which works through enhancing brain noradrenalin activity, thus indicating "the possibility of dysfunction of other neuronal systems in addition to the serotonergic system." Van Hiele comments that, "after successful [5-HTP] medication a mood level and stability are attained which the patient has not known for years. . . . It is no exaggeration to say that the patient feels like a reborn individual." Van Hiele concludes his report with much praise for 5-HTP: "I have never in 20 years used an agent which: (1) was effective so quickly; (2) restored the patients so completely to the persons they had been; (3) was so entirely without side effects; (4) failed so completely in about 50 percent of depressions, which may have been of a different biochemical type . . . (6) could have so strong a prophylactic [preventive] effect."

The last major study to be examined here is the 1991 Pöldinger report, which many consider the best study yet done on 5-HTP vs. depression.[10] Pöldinger and his fellow Swiss psychiatrists carefully assessed and treated 63 depressed patients with either 5-HTP (100 mg three times daily with meals) or fluvoxamine, a major SSRI drug (50 mg three times daily with meals), in a double-blind trial. Thirty-four patients received 5-HTP, 29 got fluvoxamine (FLUV);

32 of the 34 on 5-HTP were diagnosed with major depression, while 28 of 29 in the FLUV group suffered major depression. Most in either group had previously suffered from depression. Twenty-nine of the 5-HTP group were evaluated as having moderate to very severe depression at the onset of the study, while 20 of 29 in the FLUV group suffered moderate to very severe depression. The mean Hamilton Depression Rating Score was higher for the 5-HTP group at baseline. Both treatment groups showed gradual reduction in the depression scores after two, four, and six weeks of treatment, at which point the values were almost identical. There was a 60.7 percent decrease from beginning scores for the 5-HTP patients, vs. a 56.1 percent reduction in depression scores in the FLUV-treated patients. Analyzing the scores to focus on specific components of the depressions showed 5-HTP to have a superior percentage decrease in scores relating to depressive mood (65.7 vs. 61.8 percent), anxiety (58.2 vs. 48.3 percent), bodily pains (47.6 vs. 37.8 percent) and insomnia (61.7 vs. 55.9 percent). Within each group the decrease in Hamilton Depression scores from baseline to end was highly statistically significant. The psychiatrists conducting the tests also made ratings of each patient as to how well they had responded to treatment, without knowing who was getting 5-HTP or FLUV. In the 5-HTP group, 15 patients were evaluated as showing very good treatment response, 12 as moderate to good, and 2 as failures. In the FLUV group, the ratings were 13 patients very good, 10 moderate to good, and 5 failures. Thus the treatment failure rate with 5-HTP was 5.9 percent compared to 17.2 percent in the FLUV patients. A major contrast between 5-HTP and FLUV treatment occurred when side effects were examined. Fourteen of 34 patients (38.9 percent) in the 5-HTP group and 18 of 29 patients (54.5 percent) in the FLUV group reported 43 and 50 "adverse events" respectively. Seventeen of 34 side effects (39.6 percent) in the 5-HTP group were rated moderate or severe, while 38 of 50 side effects (76 percent) in the FLUV group were classed moderate or severe. Most of the 5-HTP side effects were various forms of gastrointestinal upset and they occurred mostly in the first two weeks of treatment. In the FLUV group intestinal upset and weakness, fatigue, and debility were the predominant side effects. Only one of the 36 5-HTP patients starting the study left because of adverse side effects (3 percent), while 4 of 33 of those beginning the study on FLUV withdrew because of adverse side effects (12 percent). Overall, the investigators in the

Pöldinger study rated 5-HTP as equal or superior to the standard SSRI antidepressant drug, fluvoxamine. Pöldinger and colleagues conclude that "supported by the results of previous studies, the outcome of the present trial should warrant 5-HTP being admitted to the core group of routinely applied antidepressive drugs."

5-HTP AND DOPAMINE/NORADRENALIN

While there is no question that a significant portion of human depression results from difficulties with brain serotonin metabolism/neurotransmission, serotonin neural circuits are not the only ones involved in depression. According to Willner, "The major changes in neurotransmission associated with severe depressions are (1) a reduced level of DA [dopamine] function, related to psychomotor [movement] retardation, and reflecting a reduced level of incentive motivation; (2) a retarded level of 5-HTP [serotonin] function, related to psychomotor agitation, and reflecting an inability to relax; (3) a reduced level of NA [noradrenalin] function . . . reflecting inability to maintain effort; and (4) cholinergic [acetylcholine] hyperactivity . . . reflecting a high level of stress. Antidepressants reverse these changes, primarily by actions on NA and 5-HTP neurons."[26]

Ironically, there are indications scattered throughout the psychobiology literature that one of the major differences between tryptophan and 5-HTP supplements, is their differential action toward the catecholamine (DA and NA) neurotransmitter systems. In many ways serotonin circuits have inhibitory effects, acting like the brakes on a car, while DA and NA circuits are the "get up and go" systems, more like the gas pedal in a car. Yet as Agren notes, "Serotonin has been thought to act as an inhibitory neurotransmitter in the cerebral cortex but, depending on which receptor is activated, it can also initiate excitation."[30] In 1986 Agren and his group reported their results from a detailed and sophisticated mathematical study on correlations between serotonin and DA levels in humans.[32] The Agren group examined CSF data from 175 humans, as well as serotonin and DA levels in 20 different brain regions of healthy dogs. In the humans, CSF levels of the chief metabolites of serotonin (5-HIAA) and dopamine (HVA-homovanillic acid) were examined. In the dog studies, actual brain levels of serotonin/DA and 5-HIAA/HVA were measured. The group concluded that, "results confirm a facilatory effect of serotonin on indices of dopamine turnover in many brain regions, especially the brain stem and hypothalamus." Thus the action of serotonin circuits is not merely that of a brake. Rather, serotonin circuits act more like a homeostatic governor or normalizer that serves to prevent DA/NA circuits from getting either excessively hyperactive (as in mania or uncontrollable violence) or excessively hypoactive (as in severe depression).

In 1975, Takahashi and colleagues conducted a small two-week study of the effects of 300 mg 5-HTP administered daily to 24 depressed patients.[33] They found a "marked" positive response to 5-HTP in seven patients, and a "mild" response in two, based on changes in Hamilton Depression Scores. The researchers might have concluded that the positive results were merely due to placebo effect, given the only one in three success rate. However when they looked at CSF data taken before and after treatment, a clear distinction between the responders and nonresponders was evident.

The researchers obtained CSF 5-HIAA and HVA levels for the 24 depressed patients just before treatment, and compared the levels to those found in 24 neurological patients matched for age and sex. The average 5-HIAA level in the neurological control group was 30.3 ng/ml, while the depressed patients had average CSF 5-HIAA levels of 19.6 ng/ml. The difference between the two groups was statistically significant. The control group averaged HVA levels of 36.8 ng/ml, while the depressed patients had similar HVA levels of 33.1 ng/ml. The difference in the two groups' HVA levels were not significant. And just as CSF 5-HIAA levels are considered crude but relevant indicators of brain serotonin activity, so CSF HVA levels are considered crude but useful reflectors of brain DA activity.[34]

After the two week trial of 5-HTP, Takahashi measured the CSF 5-HIAA and HVA in all 24 patients again. The results from the nine responders were compared to those from the 15 nonresponders. Ironically, the nonresponder group had a 42 percent increase from their baseline CSF 5-HIAA levels, while the nine 5-HTP-responders only had a 21 percent CSF 5-HIAA increase from their baseline levels. However, the nine responders had started with a higher baseline level of 5-HIAA, so their actual final 5-HIAA levels were higher than the nonresponders (27 ng/ml vs. 25.6 ng/ml). The real difference between the two groups showed up when HVA levels were compared. The nine 5-HTP-responders had their HVA levels increase over 100 percent—from 29.0 to 59.5 ng/ml. The nonresponders actually had a slight (nonsignificant) drop in HVA, from 35.4 to 33.4 ng/ml. The Takahashi group speculated that the major improvement in depression shown by the 5-HTP-responders was due more to an increase in brain dopamine activity (as reflected by the 100 percent HVA increase) than to the slight increase in serotonin activity. Yet, as the van Praag and de Haan study discussed earlier shows (and many other studies have verified this), a good response to 5-HTP, even in behavioral/emotional indices that clearly reflect improved serotonin activity, will often not be reflected in increased CSF 5-HIAA levels after 5-HTP. So Takahashi's group is doubtless right that the 5-HTP-increased dopamine activity in the nine responders contributed to their improvement, but wrong in assuming that serotonin played no role. Given the Agren study on serotonin "controlling" brain dopamine activity, the Takahashi study indicates that 5-HTP may work best as an antidepressant when it increases brain serotonin activity in a way that also "jump starts" deficient brain DA function. The most severe depressions are generally called "retarded" depressions, where a person has no energy or motivation, and even talks, thinks, moves and reacts in "slow motion." A retarded depression is the "I can't even get out of bed" variety. And van Praag and Korf (and others) have shown CSF HVA to be low in retarded depressions, indicating low brain DA activity.

Van Praag has also studied CSF metabolite levels in response to 5-HTP and tryptophan supplements. He measured the CSF responses to 200 mg 5-HTP given as both a single dose, and for one week. He also did a similar trial using 5 grams of tryptophan given as a single dose, and for one week. His results showed a clear difference between the effect of 5-HTP and tryptophan. 5-HTP caused significant increases not only in post-probenecid CSF 5-HIAA levels, but also in CSF HVA (the DA metabolite) and MHPG (the CSF metabolite of brain NA). The 5-gram tryptophan dose increased CSF 5-HIAA levels as expected, although only about 60–80 percent as much as did 5-HTP. However, the tryptophan caused no significant increase in CSF HVA or MHPG levels.

Van Praag then compared CSF metabolite levels in depressed patients whose positive response to 5-HTP continued unabated, to those in depressed patients whose favorable response to 5-HTP diminished after three to six weeks. Both groups initially showed similar increases in CSF 5-HIAA, HVA and MHPG in response to

5-HTP treatment, thus showing increased brain serotonin, DA and NA activity. When the CSF levels were measured in both groups after the effect of 5-HTP had begun to diminish in the second group, an obvious difference emerged. The group whose positive 5-HTP response continued unchanged, also showed similar continuing higher-than-baseline levels of 5-HIAA, HVA and MHPG. In the group of patients whose 5-HTP response had dropped, their CSF 5-HIAA levels remained high, but their previously 5-HTP-increased CSF HVA and MHPG levels had now dropped back down almost to their pretreatment levels. In the diminished 5-HTP response group, Hamilton Depression Scores had dropped from 28 at the beginning of 5-HTP treatment, to 18 at week two, and down to 7 by week four of 5-HTP treatment. Their scores returned to 19 after six weeks of 5-HTP treatment, when CSF tests showed they had lost their original CSF HVA and MHPG gains.[35,36] These results demonstrate that in some people 5-HTP will increase not only brain serotonin activity, but also brain DA and NA function as well. They also demonstrate that in some people the DA/NA effects may be short-lived, and that some of the antidepressant activity of 5-HTP might then be diminished.

Byerley and his colleagues also describe the DA/NA enhancing effects of 5-HTP in their 1987 review article on 5-HTP and depression.[37] They note that, "in laboratory animals as well as human subjects, increased turnover of dopamine and norephinephrine occurs after 5-HTP administration. . . . Formation of serotonin in catecholaminergic [DA/NA] neurons may alter their activity. Studies in laboratory animals, however, indicate that 5-HTP is taken up by [DA/NA] neurons only after large doses are given. Administration of 5-HTP may also affect [DA/NA] activity by virtue of its affects on serotonin metabolism. Since many synaptic connections exist between serotonergic and [DA/NA] systems in the brain, it is likely that enhancement of serotonergic activity will lead to adaptations in [DA/NA] pathways."

The message to be drawn from these studies on the DA/NA effects of 5-HTP and the lack of effect of tryptophan on DA/NA is very simple. One must be cautious in extrapolating results from studies which use tryptophan to a presumed similar action with 5-HTP. 5-HTP is not just quantitatively different from tryptophan (more potent, milligram for milligram), but may sometimes be qualitatively different (in type or kind) in its effect as well.

5-HTP AND ANXIETY

Anxiety is another emotional state that animal and human research indicates is related to serotonin nerve dysfunction. Anxiety may be experienced in a "pure form" in the classical anxiety disorders, such as panic attacks, generalized anxiety disorder, and obsessive-compulsive disorder. Anxiety is also routinely a symptom of depression—two of the 21 items measured in the Hamilton Depression Score refer to emotional and bodily anxiety symptoms. Anxiety may also be associated with severe or chronic stress, and may even manifest as ordinary "stage fright."

A few studies have used 5-HTP to treat panic disorder. In 1985 Kahn and Westenberg used 150–300 mg 5-HTP daily combined with a peripheral decarboxylase inhibitor (PDI) for 12 weeks to treat panic disorder in ten people.[38] Five of the patients complained of a mild but noticeable increase in anxiety, combined with a slight increase in frequency and severity of panic attacks during the first 10–14 days, followed by a significant improval in both generalized anxiety and panic attacks. Kahn and Westenberg confirmed these results in a larger study in 1987, comparing 5-HTP and the TCA clomipramine to placebo, with again about half of the 5-HTP group experiencing a transitory worsening of their anxiety and panic attacks followed by clinical improvement.[39]

In 1990, den Boer and Westenberg tested 20 panic disorder patients along with 20 healthy controls using 60 mg intravenously infused 5-HTP.[40] Because of the excessively high blood levels of 5-HTP generated through its direct infusion into the bloodstream, some brief side effects were noted in both patients and controls in the three hour test. Nausea and vomiting occurred in nine of the patients and 14 of the controls. Irritability, sleepiness and depression were noted in some of the controls, while disorientation and a sense of detachment from reality occurred in some patients. Again, these symptoms were attributed to the intravenous use of

5-HTP. Yet there was no significant increase in anxiety in either patients or controls, as measured by the Acute Panic Inventory (API), and the patients' API scores were actually lower three hours after 5-HTP infusion. Two of the patients reported that they felt in a better mood, nine of the patients reported feeling less anxious, and two patients said they felt "better than ever."

Depression studies have also routinely reported anxiety reductions in patients given 5-HTP. In the 1991 Pöldinger study the emotional anxiety scores in the 5-HTP group dropped 58 percent in six weeks, while the bodily anxiety symptoms scores dropped 53 percent on average.[10] In the Kaneko depression study using 5-HTP, it was remarked that "the depressive mood was ameliorated first, then anxiety, agitation, and psychomotor retardation followed in that order."[27]

In the Zmilacher study using 5-HTP both with and without a PDI, 5-HTP produced good or very good improvement in 5 of 6 patients suffering from "anxious-agitated" depression.[6] Another finding from the Zmilacher study also sheds light on the 1985 and 1987 5-HTP/panic disorder studies discussed previously. None of the 13 Zmilacher patients treated with 5-HTP **alone** suffered any acute anxiety reactions, while 4 of the 13 patients receiving 5-HTP combined with a PDI dropped out of the study due to acute anxiety attacks. One of the patients in their study was treated first with 5-HTP alone for four weeks, then with 5-HTP plus PDI. This patient exhibited no anxiety symptoms on 5-HTP alone, but developed acute anxiety attacks when switched to the 5-HTP/PDI combination. Thus the brief initial worsening of anxiety seen in the two panic disorder studies may have arisen from the PDI component of treatment, rather than the 5-HTP itself.

Willner reported that a serotonin synthesis inhibitor, PCPA, which blocks conversion of tryptophan to 5-HTP, was given to six normal volunteers, 22 medical patients and one opiate addict.[26] A PCPA-induced 60–80 percent reduction of serotonin function produced restlessness, anxiety and agitation, further demonstrating the 5-HTP-serotonin-anxiety connection. Willner also points out that "5-HTP [serotonin] depletion in animals results in aggression, hyperemotionality, and hyperreactivity to pain or threat. In people, low 5-HTP turnover is associated with anxiety, agitation, and aggression. . . . In both cases, the syndrome may be summarized in one word—irritability."[26]

5-HTP, APPETITE CONTROL AND WEIGHT REDUCTION

Over the past 25 years, a wealth of data from human and animal studies has confirmed that brain serotonin has a primary inhibitory role in regulating eating behavior in both animals and humans, and in producing satiety after eating. In 1975 Blundell and Lesham reported a significant reduction in food intake in obese rats prone to overeating when the animals were given 5-HTP injections.[41] In 1982 it was confirmed that Osborne-Mendell rats, which are genetically predisposed to obesity, have abnormally decreased brain tryptophan hydroxylase (TH) activity. TH is the enzyme that converts tryptophan to 5-HTP. 5-HTP injected in microamounts into the brains of rats reduces feeding, while brain injection of PCPA, a serotonin synthesis inhibitor, increases feeding.

The recently recalled diet drugs, Pondimin® and Redux®, both work by releasing serotonin and preventing its reuptake in brain neurons. Studies reported by Dr. J. Wurtman in 1988 showed that Redux suppressed snack intake by carbohydrate (CHO) cravers, but not in non-CHO cravers.[42] In 1988, Lyons and Truswell reported their results comparing high CHO breakfasts with high protein breakfasts.[43] A high sugar breakfast raised the blood tryptophan ratio from 0.10 to 0.133 and a high starch breakfast increased the ratio from 0.106 to 0.127, while a high protein breakfast dropped the ratio from 0.106 to 0.057. The high CHO meals would thus raise brain tryptophan levels, while the high protein meal would lower brain tryptophan. And in 1990, Drs. Schaechter and Wurtman reported evidence that brain tryptophan (or 5-HTP) levels would determine neuronal serotonin levels, and that the synaptic release of serotonin would be proportional to the levels of intracellular serotonin.[44]

Judith Wurtman also reported the results of a study with 150 obese people who claimed snacking as the cause of their obesity.[42] Many of those studied routinely experienced episodes of CHO-craving in late afternoon or evening. During such CHO-binges, more than 800 calories of starchy and sweet foods (bagels, crackers, cookies) were eaten. Despite easy access during the study to alternative high protein snack foods (cheese, cold meats, chicken and tuna salad), the study subjects persistently ate only CHO snack foods. Subsequent studies with CHO-cravers showed that they intentionally overate snack CHOs (irrespective of sweetness) because they correctly anticipated a desired mood lift from CHO foods. For those people, CHO-rich foods act as a mild form of serotonin self-medication. (See Blundell[41]; Cangiano[11]; Ceci[45];Welt-zin[46]; Willner[26]; and Wurtman 1988[42] on the serotonin-eating control connection.)

Based on the prior animal and human data, the Italian group of Cangiano, Ceci and associates conducted two studies on the effects of 5-HTP in appetite and weight control.[11,45] Their first study was a double-blind crossover study with 19 obese females who were given either 5-HTP (3.6 mg/pound bodyweight/day) or a placebo for five weeks. After a one week delay, the 5-HTP and placebo groups were reversed. No dietary restrictions were prescribed. The average daily food intake was 2,903 calories/day at baseline. The placebo group spontaneously dropped their calorie intake 20 percent, to 2,327, over the five-week study, while the 5-HTP group dropped 37 percent, to 1,819 cal/day. Both groups showed a similarly modest drop in protein intake, from 101 grams/day to 85 gms/day (placebo) and 79 gms/day (5-HTP). The big food decrease was in CHOs—the 5-HTP group dropped from 274 gms CHO/day to 176 gms CHO/day, a 36 percent decrease. This presumably reflected the lessened need for CHOs to enhance brain tryptophan uptake, since 5-HTP was now available to enhance brain serotonin synthesis. The 5-HTP group also showed a statistically significant weight loss (3.3 lbs) compared to the placebo group (0.9 lbs).

Ceci and Cangiano's next study was a 12-week double-blind study, completed by 20 obese women.[11] Half received 300mg 5-HTP three times per day, 30 minutes before each meal. In the first 6 weeks no diet was prescribed; during the second 6 weeks a 1200 calorie diet was prescribed. The placebo group dropped from a baseline 2,732 cal/day to 2,336 cal/day at 6 weeks, and further to 2,065 cal/day during the prescribed diet period. Neither decrease was statistically significant. The 5-HTP group started at a higher 3,232 cal/day food intake, dropping to 1,886 cal/day after 6 weeks, a highly significant decrease of 42 percent. During the diet period the 5-HTP group further decreased to an average 1,273 cal/day, a further 33 percent drop from the week-6 level. There were no statistically significant decreases from baseline in protein, CHO or fat intake in the placebo group, either at week 6 or week 12. The 5-HTP group significantly lowered protein intake from about 115 to 70 gm/day at week 6, with protein intake reaching a plateau thereafter. They also significantly lowered fat intake, from 150 gm/

day at baseline, to 90 gm/day at week 6 and 50 gm/day at week 12. The 5-HTP group also showed a massive drop in CHO intake, from 350 gm/day at baseline, to 210 gm/day at week 6 and 150 gm/day at week 12. The placebo group lost only a statistically insignificant two pounds of weight over the whole 12 weeks. The 5-HTP group lost four pounds during the 6-week initial period, and seven more pounds during the 6-week prescribed diet period, representing a highly significant weight loss.

Both Ceci/Cangiano studies measured emotional states and satiety levels using various questionnaires.[11,45] No significant mood changes were reported during the studies, but the 5-HTP group did show evidence of increased satiety from eating, which seemed to reduce the urge to eat.

It should be noted that both studies used 5-HTP capsules with a special enteric coating that would not dissolve until the capsule passed through the stomach into the intestine. This was based on van Praag's observations that risk and/or intensity of gastric upset from 5-HTP could be reduced by such capsules. A peripheral decarboxylase inhibitor (PDI) was not used in either study. The use of such a high dose of 5-HTP, taken on an empty stomach and without such enteric coating, would be highly likely to cause significant gastric distress, and is not recommended.

Cangiano and colleagues conclude their second study with the statement that, "the administration of 5-HTP was in fact followed by a reduction of both daily total energy and carbohydrate intakes followed by a significant loss of body weight. The optimal adherence to dietary prescription as well as the good tolerance to 5-HTP treatment observed suggest that this substance may be safely used in the long-term treatment of obesity."

SEROTONIN AND PMS

Research done in the 1980s strongly suggests a serotonin link to PMS—premenstrual syndrome.[42,47] Richard and Judith Wurtman and coworkers reported the results of their research comparing the incidence of CHO-craving, mood and eating behavior among 19 PMS patients and 9 control subjects. The test subjects were admitted to the MIT Research Center for 48 hours during two different menstrual phases—the follicular (4–7 days postmenstruation) and the late luteal phase (3–5 days before menstruation). Meal calorie and nutrient intake were carefully measured, and test subjects also had access to high CHO and high protein snacks (equal in calorie) value to choose from between meals. Mood was assessed with the Hamilton Depression Scale, combined with an additional test which evaluated fatigue, sociability, appetite and CHO-craving. During the late luteal (premenstrual) phase the PMS patients significantly increased their total calorie intake, from an average of 1892 to 2395, while CHO intake was increased 24 percent at meals and 43 percent through snacks. There was no change in protein intake. The Hamilton Depression Scores during the late luteal (premenstrual) phase in the PMS patients rose from 2.0 to 21.2, while the additional test scores rose from 0.5 to 10.2 There was no significant change in the Hamilton and additional scores among the control subjects during the premenstrual phase. Mood was assessed two hours before and after a high CHO/low protein test meal. Consumption of the test meal during the late luteal (premenstrual) phase improved scores relating to depression, tension, anger, confusion, sadness, fatigue, alertness and calmness among PMS patients, while the test meal produced no significant mood changes during the follicular phase of the menstrual cycle. The Wurtmans concluded from their study that PMS sufferers may overconsume CHOs during their premenstrual cycle in an attempt to improve their depressed/irritable mood states, presumably through the ability of 5-HTP to increase brain serotonin synthesis. Given the proven ability of 5-HTP to increase brain serotonin, PMS sufferers may now have a better alternative to weight-increasing CHO-binging to chase away their "premenstrual blues."

SAFETY OF 5-HTP

Since 5-HTP became widely available in America in 1997, various warnings and objections to the use of this supplement have circulated on the Internet and appeared in several magazine articles. What are these objections, and are they any cause for concern over 5-HTP use?

1) Some critics have claimed that 5-HTP should be used (if at all) only with a peripheral decarboxylase inhibitor (PDI). Otherwise, it is claimed, most or all of the 5-HTP will be converted to serotonin outside the brain; and since serotonin does not pass the blood-brain barrier, any hoped for benefit from 5-HTP would be nullified. Yet when Dr. Zmilacher and associates reviewed 17 5-HTP studies, they found that 5-HTP was more effective (64 percent) in the studies that did not use a PDI, than in the studies that did (52.9 percent). Zmilacher's own study also found more and more severe, side effects when 5-HTP was combined with a PDI.[6] Furthermore, studies infusing tryptophan or 5-HTP directly into the bloodstream have been done, and they did not show any significant increase in blood serontonin caused by increased blood 5-HTP. Thus, Dr. Li Kam Wa and associates report that, "Six healthy male subjects received . . . 5-hydroxy-L-tryptophan (5-HTP) . . . on two occasions in a randomized crossover study. There were marked increases in urinary 50-HTP and 5-HT [serotonin] excretion after infusion of 5-HTP. . . . This occurred without significant changes in blood 5-HT levels measured in platelet rich plasma . . ."[48] Huether's report on tryptophan infusion in 14 healthy young men states that "5-hydroxy-Trp [5-HTP] rose rapidly and massively after Trp [tryptophan] infusions . . . more than 20-fold . . . and declined rapidly to about 5-fold baseline levels within 2 h. Whole blood serotonin levels were

almost unaffected by the Trp infusions in spite of the massive rise in blood 5-HTP induced by the tryptophan."[49] Thus, both clinical studies and blood serotonin measurements in response to dramatically increased blood 5-HTP levels fail to support the claim that 5-HTP without PDI will only elevate blood serotonin and not brain serotonin.

II) Some people have claimed that the high blood levels of serotonin allegedly resulting from using 5-HTP without a PDI, would cause blood platelets to form clots and trigger a heart attack, or cause a spasm of the heart arteries—coronary artery vasospasm—which would also trigger a heart attack. If this were true, there would be reports of such results in the literature—but there are not. It is true that serotonin can play a role in blood platelet aggregation, and arterial constriction as well. However, the evidence presented to answer objection I) makes it clear that 5-HTP supplements don't raise blood serotonin. The many test subjects receiving 5-HTP over the past 30 years should have suffered numerous heart attacks if this objection were true—yet nowhere is this mentioned in the vast literature on human 5-HTP use. As Byerley and colleagues note in their major review article on 5-HTP use: "Researchers who reported on the results of various laboratory functions (hematologic [i.e. blood], liver, kidney, etc.) found that 5-HTP caused no significant changes. . . . Oral administration of 5-HTP, with or without a PDI, is associated with few adverse effects."[37]

III) Some have claimed that Americans' use of vitamin B6 supplements can increase 5-HTP's (alleged) problems, since B6 activates the enzyme LAAD that could convert 5-HTP to serotonin in the bloodstream. Yet, as Hartvig points out, experiments with monkeys given B6 intravenously along with 5-HTP, and rats fed "moderate excess" amounts of B6, increased brain serotonin production up to 60 percent—an impossible finding if B6 caused the bulk of ingested 5-HTP to convert to serotonin outside the brain.[3] And the College Pharmacy of Colorado, a major mail-order compounding pharmacy, has sold (by prescription) a product with 100mg 5-HTP and 12.5 mg B6 (without PDI) since 1990 with no problems.

IV) Some critics offer the scenario that a relatively rare type of serotonin-secreting tumor, called "hind-gut carcinoid," may also be associated with heart-valve damage and heart failure, and then claim this somehow proves no one should use 5-HTP. Of course, such warnings offer no evidence (and don't really claim, but merely imply) that taking 5-HTP at reasonable doses would actually cause these tumors, or the heart damage sometimes associated with them. And many reports on this "carcinoid syndrome" acknowledge that there is no clear evidence that the high blood-serotonin levels found in the syndrome cause the heart problems. Thus cardiologist Dr. L. Lundin wrote in 1991: "Several substances known to be released from carcinoid tumors have been proposed as possible mediators of the cardiac pathology in carcinoid heart disease, e.g. vasoactive substances such as serotonin and bradykinin, but no causal relationship has yet been found."[50] Arora and Warner concluded that, "unlike the animal model, our data failed to demonstrate a difference in blood tryptophan, serotonin, or [5-HIAA] levels with or without cardiac involvement. This suggests that other chemical mediators besides [serotonin], perhaps bradykinin, may play a role in the pathogenesis of endocardial injury."[51] And Dr. K. Tornebrandt and his fellow M.D.s reached the conclusion that, "although the heart lesions have been attributed to high levels of 5-HT [serotonin], we did not find any correlation between the measured high levels of blood 5-HT or urinary 5-HIAA levels and the degree of heart involvement."[52] Carcinoid syndrome thus has no bearing on the issue of general 5-HTP safety, although prudence suggests those individuals suffering from metastatic carcinoid disease should only use 5-HTP with their physician's recommendation and supervision.

V) Some critics have claimed that 5-HTP is safe to use only if regular urine tests are done and the urinary 5-HIAA level remains low. Yet many studies *safely* using 5-HTP have found high urinary 5-HIAA. For example, the 1989 Ceci and 1992 Cangiano studies both used high dose 5-HTP, and reported 5-HIAA urinary levels 50 times higher in the 5-HTP group compared to placebo group levels.[11,45] And both reports ended with a statement extolling the safety of 5-HTP for long-term obesity treatment.

VI) One critic has attacked 5-HTP use on the grounds that it will (allegedly) only increase serotonin activity in the brain, and that this will cause the brain to shut down production of serotonin (down-regulate it) and thus inhibit total brain function. This complaint simply ignores the widespread acknowledgment in the 5-HTP psychobiology literature that 5-HTP/serotonin frequently acts to up-regulate brain dopamine/noradrenalin activity, as discussed earlier in this booklet. And van Hiele has reported that many of his patients returned to normal job and family life through 5-HTP use, after an average 7–10-years-long therapy-resistant severe depression, which hardly sounds like "serotonin brain shut-down." While some researchers have found 5-HTP more effective in the anxious-agitated-irritable type depression, many have also reported success in at least some of the retarded, vegetative "can't get out of bed" type depressions. For more detail on 5-HTP's brain dopamine/noradrenalin activating effect, the reader is referred to Agren[32], Byerley[7], van Praag[35,36] and Willner.[26]

HOW TO USE 5-HTP SUPPLEMENTS

The clinical literature on 5-HTP provides some guidelines for use, but in the end each person will need to find the best way to use 5-HTP. Some people have reported that taking 5-HTP in the daytime may briefly make them drowsy or lethargic, while others have noted that daytime 5-HTP simply "mellows their mood" in spite of the stresses of the day. Some people take 5-HTP only once daily, at bedtime, and report this both aids good sleep and still helps them cope with stress more cheerfully the next day. The clinical literature recommends starting with a modest dose—25–50 mg—and only slowly increasing dosage if necessary, in order to minimize the risk and/or severity of possible gastrointestinal (GI) upset. Taking 5-HTP with food, partway through a meal or snack, is also suggested to minimize possible GI symptoms. In the many human depression studies using 5-HTP, total daily 5-HTP dose is usually 200–300 mg, with occasionally even 100 mg providing positive results. Thus, for more ordinary "food supplement" uses, 50–150 mg daily will probably be an adequate dose.

Two more novel delivery forms may also provide 5-HTP benefit at lower doses while also reducing the risk of GI upset. A sublingual 5-HTP tablet containing 20 or 25 mg 5-HTP is available. The sublingual tablet is designed to dissolve slowly under the tongue—usually in one to four minutes—and the 5-HTP molecules are believed to diffuse through the top cell layers of the tongue and cheek areas into capillaries just below the surface. The molecules enter the tiny blood vessels through "slit pores" that occur along the capillaries, and then travel to the brain. The sublingual absorption method at least partially bypasses the intestine and the "first pass through the liver," where much of any 5-HTP that is swallowed would be metabolized and destroyed. Thus sublingual 5-HTP tablets may provide more brain 5-HTP benefit at a lower dose and with less GI upset risk, but results are not available to us at this writing.

A "liposome spray" form of 5-HTP has been developed to spray into the mouth and as with the sublingual tablet form, 5-HTP is believed to pass directly into the bloodstream. The spray form of 5-HTP also allows for lower dose use compared to swallowed capsules or tablets.

Those who might be concerned with a possible repeat of the tryptophan problem of 1989 will be relieved to know that 5-HTP is manufactured by a completely different method. At that time, the FDA took tryptophan off the market after a bad batch was produced by a single Japanese manufacturer. The tryptophan that caused many people to become sick and so to die was manufactured through bacterial fermentation. A minor contaminant produced by the bacteria was not removed when the producer eliminated some filtration steps traditionally used to purify the bacterial product. 5-HTP is extracted from the seed of a West African legume, *Griffonia simplicifolia*, and has been in safe use in Europe for over 20 years.

SELECTED REFERENCES

1. Robertson, J. with Monte, T. (1997). *Natural Prozac*. S.F.: Harper.
2. Young, S. N. (1991). Some effects of dietary components (amino acids, carbohydrates, folic acid) on brain serotonin synthesis, mood and behavior. *Can J Physiol Pharmacol*, 69, 893–903.
3. Hartvig, P., Lindner, K. J. et al. (1995). Pyridoxine effect on synthesis rate of serotonin in the monkey brain measured with PET. *J Neural Transm* (Gen Sect), 102, 91–97.
4. Kant, A. K. and Block, G. (1990). Dietary vitamin B-6 intake and food sources in the US population. *Am J Clin Nutr*, 52, 707–716.
5. Slutsker, L. Hoesley, F. C. et al. (1990). Eosiniphilia-myalgia syndrome associated with exposure to tryptophan from a single manufacturer. *JAMA*, 264, 213–217.
6. Zmilacher, K., Battegay, R. and Gastpar, M. (1988). L-5-hydroxytryptophan alone and in combination with a peripheral decarboxylase inhibitor in the treatment of depression. *Neuropsychobiol*, 20, 28–35.
7. Byerley, W. F. and Risch, S. C. (1985). Depression and serotonin metabolism: rationale for neurotransmitter precursor treatment. *J Clin Psychopharmac*, 5, 191–206.
8. Cooper, J. R., Bloom, F. E. and Roth, R. H. (1996). *The Biochemical Basis of Neuropharmacology*, NY, Oxford: Oxford Univ. Press, p. 359.
9. Julien, R. M. (1995). *A Primer of Drug Action*. NY: W. H. Freeman. pp. 93–197; 204–205.
10. Pöldinger, W., Calanchini, B. & Schwarz, W. (1991). A functional-dimensional approach to depression: serotonin deficiency as a target syndrome in a comparison of 5-hydroxytryptophan and fluvoxamine. *Psychopathol*, 24, 53–81.
11. Cangiano, C., Ceci, F. et al. (1992). Eating behavior and adherence to dietary prescriptions in obese adult subjects treated with 5-hydroxytryptophan. *Am J Clin Nutr*, 56, 863–867.
12. van Hiele, L. J. (1980). L-5-hydroxytryptophan in depression: the first substitution therapy in psychiatry? *Neuropsychobiol*, 6, 230–240.
13. van Praag, H. M. and Korf, J. (1973). Cerebral monoamines and depression. *Arch Gen Psychiat*, 28, 827–831.

14. Delgado, P. L., Charney, D. S. et al. (1990). Serotonin function and the mechanism of antidepressant action. *Arch Gen Psychiat*, 47, 411–418.
15. Lopez-Ibor, J. J., Gutierrez, J. J. A. and Iglesias, M. L. M. (1976). 5-hydroxytryptophan (5-HTP) and a MAOI (Nialamide) in the treatment of depression. *Int J Pharmacopsychiat*, 11, 8–15.
16. Mendelwicz, J. and Youdin, M. B. H. (1980). Antidepressant potentiation of 5-hydroxytryptophan by L-deprenyl in affective illness. *J Affect Disord*, 2, 137–146.
17. van Praag, H. M, van den Burg, W. et al. (1974). 5-hydroxytryptophan in combination with clomipramine in "therapy-resistant" depression. *Psychopharmac* (Berlin), 38, 267–269.
18. Sternbach, H. (1991). The serotonin syndrome. *Am J Psychiat*, 148, 505–513.
19. Stahl, S. M. (1996). *Essential Psychopharmacologoy*. Cambridge: Cambridge Univ Press. Pp. 100–106.
20. Charney, E. A. and Weissman, M. M. (1988). Epidemiology of depressive and manic syndromes. In A. Gerogotas & R. Cancro (Eds.), *Depression and mania* (26–52). NY: Elsevier.
21. van Praag, H. M. (1981). Management of depression with serotonin precursors. *Biol Psychiat*, 16, 291–310.
22. Thompson, J., Rankin, H. et al. (1982). The treatment of depression in general practice: a comparison of L-tryptophan, amitriptyline, and a combination of L-tryptophan and amitriptyline, with placebo. *Psychol Med*, 12, 741–751.
23. Persson, T. and Roos, B. E. (1967). 5-hydroxytryptophan for depression. *Lancet*, II, 987–988.
24. Sano, I. (1972). L-5-hydroxytryptophan (L-5HTP) therapie. *Folia Psychiat Neurol Jpn*, 26, 7–17.
25. van Praag, H. M. & Korf, J. et al. (1972). A pilot study of the predictive value of the probenecid test in application of 5-hydroxytryptophan as antidepressant. *Psychopharmac* (Berlin), 25, 14–21.
26. Willner, P. (1985). *Depression—A Psychobiological Synthesis*. NY: Johnn Wiley, PP. 310, 317, 325, 375.
27. Kaneko, M., Kumashiro, H. et al. (1979). L-5-HTP treatment and serum 5 HT level after L-5-HTP loading on depressed patients. *Neuropsychobiol*, 5, 232–240.
28. Magnussen, I. & deFine Olivarius, B. (1978). Absorption deficiency of 5-hydroxy-L-tryptophan during long-term treatment in man. *Prog NeuroPsychopharmac*, 3, 395–396.
29. Westenberg, H. G. M., Gerritsen, T. W. et al. (1982). Kinetics of L-5-hydroxytryptophan in healthy subjects. *Psychiat Res*, 7, 373–385.
30. Agren, H., Reibring, L. et al. (1991). Low brain uptake of L- [11C] 5-hydroxytryptophan in major depression: a PET study on patients and healthy volunteers. *Acta Psychiatr Scand*, 83, 449–455.

31. van Praag, H. M. and de Haan, S. (1980). Depression vulnerability and 5-hydroxytryptophan prophylaxis. *Psychiat Res*, 3, 75–83.
32. Agren, H., Mefford, I. N. et al. (1986). Interacting neurotransmitter systems. *J Psychiat Res*, 20, 175–193.
33. Takahashi, S., Kondo, H. and Kato, N. (1975). Effect of L-5-hydroxy-tryptophanon brain monoamine metabolism and evaluation of its clinical effect in depressed patients. *J Psychiat Res*, 12, 177–187.
34. van Praag, H. M. and Korf, J. (1971). Retarded depression and the dopamine metabolism. *Psychopharmac* (Berlin), 19, 199–203.
35. van Praag, H. M. (1983). In search of the mode of action of antidepresssants. *Neuropharmac*, 22, 433–440.
36. van Praag, H. M. (1984). Studies in the mechanism of action of serotonin precursors in depression. *Psychopharmac Bull*, 20, 599–602.
37. Byerley, W. F., Judd, L. L. et al. (1987). 5-hydroxytryptophan: a review of its antidepressant efficacy and adverse effects. *J Clin Psychopharmac*, 7, 127–137.
38. Kahn, R. S. & Westenberg, H. G. M. (1985). L-5-hydroxytryptophan in the treatment of anxiety disorders. *J Affect Disord*, 8, 197–200.
39. Kahn, R. S., Westenberg, H. G. M. et al. (1987). Effect of a serotonin precursor and uptake inhibitor in anxiety disorders. *Int Clin Psychopharmac*, 2, 33–45.
40. den Boer, J. A. and Westenberg, H. G. M. (1990). Behavioral, neuroendocrine, and biochemical effects of 5-hydroxytryptophan administration in panic disorder. *Psychiat Res*, 31, 267–278.
41. Blundell, J. E. and Lesham, M. B. (1975). The effect of 5-hydroxytryptophan on food intake and on the anorexic action of amphetamine and fenfluramine. *J Pharm Pharmac*, 27, 31–37.
42. Wurtman. J. J. (1988). Carbohydrate craving, mood changes and obesity. *J Clin Psychiat* (Supplement), 49, 37–39.
43. Lyons, P. M. and Truswell, A. S. (1988). Serotonin precursor influenced by type of carbohydrate meal in healthy adults. *Am J Clin Nutr*, 47, 433–39.
44. Schaechter, J. D., and Wurtman, R. J. (1990). Serotonin release varies with brain tryptophan levels. 203–210, 532.
45. Ceci, F., Cangiano, C. et al. (1989). The effects of oral 5-hydroxytryptophan administration on feeding behavior in obese adult female subjects. *J Neural Transm*, 76, 109–117.
46. Weltzin, T. E., Fernstrom, M. H. and Kaye, W. H. (1994). Serotonin and bulimia nervosa. *Nutr Rev*, 52, 399–408.
47. Wurtman, J. J., Brzezinski, A. and Wurtman, R. J. (1989). Effect of nutrient intake on premenstrual depression. *Am J Obstet Gynecol*, 161, 1228–1234.
48. Li Kam Wa, T. C., Burns, N. J. T. et al. (1995). Blood and urine 5-hydroxytryptophan and 5-hydroxtryptamine levels after administration

of two 5-hydroxytryptamine precursors in normal man. *Br J Clin Pharmac*, 39, 327–329.

49. Huether, G., Hajak, G. et al. (1992). The metabolic fate of infused L-tryptophan in men: possible clinical implications of the accumulation of circulating tryptophan and tryptophan metabolites. *Psychopharmac*, 109, 422–432.
50. Lundin, L. (1991). Carcinoid heart disease. *Acta Oncol*, 30, 499–502.
51. Arora, R. R. and Warner, R. R. P. (1986). Do indole markers predict carcinoid disease? *Chest*, 90, 87–89.
52. Tornebrandt, K., Eskilsson, J. and Nobin, A. (1986). Heart involvement in metastatic carcinoid disease. *Clin Cardiol*, 9, 13–19.